THE PALAU
DE LA
MÚSICA
CATALANA

THE PALAU DE LA MÚSICA CATALANA

JOSEP M. CARANDELL

RICARD PLA

PERE VIVAS

PALAU MÚSICA CATALANA
BARCELONA

TRIANGLE ▼ POSTALS

" NOTHING ENDS, EVERYTHING BEGINS"

This expressive line by J.V. Foix provides a fitting epigraph for our book on the Palau.

Because the Palau, as a true work of art, does not just invite multiple interpretations, it demands them, to show us its magical aura, its perennial breath of poetry.

This volume brings us an extraordinary Palau in pictures: outstanding not just for the subject matter but for the sensitivity with which it has been treated. A veritable exercise in re-creation!

©   TRIANGLE POSTALS S.L.
Tel. (971) 15 04 51
Fax (971) 15 18 36
www.triangle.cat

© Text   Josep Maria Carandell

© Photographs   Ricard Pla | Pere Vivas
P. 9, Museu Nacional d'Art de Catalunya
P. 11, 13, 15, 16, 17, 149, Fundació
Orfeó Català-Palau de la Música Catalana
360-degree panoramic views   Juanjo Puente

Design   Joan Barjau
Layout   Mercè Camerino | Antonio G. Funes
Translation   David Sutcliffe | Steve Cedar

Photomechanics   Tecnoart
Printed by   Sanvergrafic
5-2010

Registration number   B: 31.110-2006
ISBN   978-84-8478-210-0

CONTENTS

LLUÍS DOMÈNECH I MONTANER

L luís Domènech i Montaner's story is quite an extraordinary one, and we can only hope to give a bare outline here. In a sense it stands on three legs like a tripod. The first leg is the career of a creative architect, who began life in 1850; the second is the happy chance meeting of two musicians in 1891, and the third is the creation of a work of architecture where the three destinies come together in a perfect, seamless whole.

Lluís Domènech i Montaner, was born on the 21 December 1850 in Barcelona. His father was a prominent book-binder and publisher, and his mother was an heiress, eldest daughter of the Montaner family of Canet de Mar.

Architecture, fine arts and culture in general, research, history and politics, Domènech i Montaner was brilliantly successful in them all.
"He was of modest stature" wrote Josep Maria Roca, "but of distinguished and slim appearance. He was a man of few words, and spoke in a shy, reserved way even to social inferiors or uneducated people. Occasionally brusque, sometimes irritable despite his shy temperament, he was, deep down, a heart that would become indignant over injustice and fill with tenderness towards the good." He qualified as an architect in Madrid and then toured Europe: in France he studied the architecture and theories of the French architect Viollet-le-Duc, and in Germany the architecture of that time, during the early days of Bismark's Reich. In Italy he went to Venice to study the ancient architecture of the city.

Soon after finishing his university career (1873) he won the chair for projects at the School of Architecture in Barcelona where he eventually became director. His article "In search of a national architecture", published in 1878, is of seminal importance in the position it takes against the eclectic mix of styles currently in vogue, and in its will to find an alternative, a new style more in key with the industrial and cultural demands of the time. Other studies brought him fame as a researcher of Catalan architecture, particularly the Romanesque style. "He was a tireless worker, and

Portrait of Lluís Domènech i Montaner, by Ramon Casas

was much more at home quietly and patiently working in museums, archives and libraries or on journeys and excursions, than in the tough, demanding atmosphere of the building sites with their workers, contractors, meetings and owners."

He founded or contributed to publications like "La Renaixença", "La Veu de Catalunya", and "El Poble Català"; he was president of the Barcelona Athenaeum, promoter and president of the Jocs Florals, or poetry contests, and member of the Acadèmia de Bones Lletres.

He soon became a prominent figure in active politics; he became president of the Catalonian League and the Catalanist Union, and one of the organisers of the assembly that approved the Bases de Manresa – the basis for a new constitution for Catalonia. He was also member of the Catalan National Centre and of the Nationalist League. He retired during the First World War, disillusioned with politics, and died in 1923.

All this was combined with his career as an architect: he launched modernist architecture and art with the Montaner i Simón building, and even more clearly with the Castell dels tres Dragons in the Parc de la Ciutadella, and the Hotel Internacional. Together with the architect Gallissà, he set up a workshop in the Castell dels tres Dragons building specialising in decorative arts applied to architecture.

His great creative period, however, was in the years on either side of the turn of the century. During this period he produced the very finest of his work, including the Institut Pere Mata, the Thomas, Navàs and Lleó Morera buildings, the Hospital de Sant Pau, and culminating in the Palau de la Música Catalana. Of all these, the Palau is the boldest and most incredibly original – it is here that the new, specifically Catalan style which Domènech i Montaner was seeking finally triumphs. The Palau won the architect an award from the Barcelona City Council in 1909. It is the synthesis of Lluís Domènech i Montaner's great architectural work.

View of the site where the Palau was built, with remains of the cloister of the convent of Sant Francesc

THE CATALAN CHORAL SOCIETY

One of the seeds planted by the Universal Exhibition of Barcelona was the idea of the Orpheon society, the choral societies that had made their appearance shortly before in France. The idea successfully took root in Catalonia when Orpheons from France and elsewhere in Europe came to take part in the choral exhibition of that auspicious year 1888. There is a precedent to all this that necessarily has to be mentioned: "La Fraternitat" choral society, afterwards known as the "Euterpe". This choir had been formed in Barcelona in 1845 by Josep Anselm Clavé to bring culture and left-wing or federal political thought into the taverns. They sang songs written by Clavé himself, first in Spanish, and then later also in Catalan – on many different themes, occasionally revolutionary.

The Orfeó Català was founded by two musicians in Barcelona in the autumn of 1891. The older of the two, Lluís Millet, had studied music with the maestro Rodoreda. He was a serious, determined young man with strong religious feelings, born in El Masnou twenty-four years earlier. The other, Amadeu Vives, born in Collbató in 1871, was "a man anatomically blighted by poliomyelitis, left crippled, lame, and gloomy of constitution", according to Sagarra in his "Memorias". But in addition to being every inch a musician, he was a man of extraordinary, nimble, caustic intelligence.

Neither of the two had met Clavé, but they did have vivid and unforgettable memories of the Choral competition at the Universal Exhibition of Barcelona. Indeed, these musical events were what inspired these two men to create a new choir that would have the rigour of refined art and the Catalan sentiments then emerging; that would revive traditional Catalan song without neglecting the great classics of sung music.

The new cultural society was founded on 6 September 1891, and its articles were passed a month later. According to the pamphlet "Orfeó Català. Historial amb motiu del XXV aniversari de sa fundació, 1891-1916" (Orfeó Català. History on the occasion of the XXV anniversary of its foun-

Laying the foundation stone, April 23, 1905

dation 1891-1916) the choir initially consisted of the two founding member-directors and 28 singers, some of whom had absolutely no musical training, and 37 patron members. What they did have was the lusty enthusiasm of youth and the self-assurance of those who know what they want. The Society had various headquarters. The first, in the Carrer Lledó, a mansion-lined street that had seen better days, where the Society rented premises, and from where they prepared for their first public appearance, under the direction of maestro Millet at the Sala Bernareggi. Afterwards, the Orpheons occupied an apartment in a building in the Carrer de Canvis Nous. At this time they had 50 choir members, but times were difficult and there were many problems, and before long they had to move to other rented premises.

In the new house in Carrer de Dufort (a street that no longer exists, near where the central Post Office now stands) the society worked hard for twelve years, achieving a series of successes at European level. There, the boys section was created, directed in its earlier years by Joan Gay, and the young ladies, organised by Emerenciana Wehrle and Josep Lapeyra.

In 1897 the society moved to the splendid Palau Moixó, in the Plaça de Sant Just i Pastor, ushering in a new and glorious chapter in their history, and for some time they took temporary premises in the Carrer de Ripoll and the Carrer de les Magdalenes, before moving once and for all to their permanent headquarters.

Main façade of building: original project

The Palau in 1908

The auditorium during the grand opening, 15 February 1908 ➲

THE PALAU AND THE NEIGHBOURHOOD OF SANT PERE

The Sant Pere district in Barcelona grew up around the track that led from the city walls to the Monastery of Sant Pere de les Puelles. At the end of the 10th century this settlement was known as Vilanova de Sant Pere.

As a district it comprises the monastery, the church and the three thoroughfares named after Sant Pere: the upper, middle and lower streets (Sant Pere més Alt, Sant Pere Mitjà and Sant Pere més Baix, respectively). There are also the narrow lanes that cross at right angles to these three. By the 14th century the neighbourhood was already the flourishing centre of the textile industry in the city. Most of the workshops and mills are gone – some as famous as the Sert family business, a family which gave Barcelona two admirable artists: the painter Josep M. Sert and architect Josep Lluís Sert. But the wholesalers and warehouses of the sector certainly are still there in force. When the city walls were demolished in the mid-nineteenth century, the industrial firms in the neighbourhood moved up into the nearby streets of the Eixample (Barcelona's 19th century Extension) and became the driving force behind the mighty Catalan industry.

When the Via Laietana, the major thoroughfare which forms the western limit of the San Pere district, was opened at the beginning of the 20th century, many streets were demolished to make way. It was on one of the resulting vacant lots that Lluís Domènech i Montaner was to build the headquarters for the Orfeó Català. At this point, Joaquim Cabot, the prominent figure in the economic and cultural affairs of the time, was president and promoter of the Society.

The first thing to note about the Palau de la Música is that it is not only an utterly strange and unusual building in itself, it is also unusual because of its setting among the buildings of a traditional inner city neighbourhood, and not alongside other modernist buildings in Barcelona's Eixample.

A balcony overlooking Sant Pere més Alt, seen from the Lluís Millet lounge

One of the immediate impressions conveyed by the Palau is that here is a building which, rather than closed in, is open on all sides, with few continuous walls.

The Palau is a perfectly harmonious marriage of different materials: the exposed brick, the glazed tiles, the glass and iron, intended to improve visibility. Not even the great sculpture group by Miquel Blay on the corner of the building makes the Palau noticeably less transparent. And this is especially evident in the entrance because, instead of our view being cut off at the vestibule as normally happens in other buildings, here our eyes are not impeded by any barrier, and our gaze loses itself in the interior. If everyone has a face, the equivalent in a building being the façade, here is a person without a face, a building without a façade, as if its very being were openness and transparency. A world of glass and glass figures. This is precisely what modernity signifies, with modernism as its prophet; this is what the building sets out to mean and succeeds in meaning.

Indeed, glass plays a very important part in the Palau, because of the many doors, windows, stained glass and, naturally, lights and reflectors. The house as a defense and protected inner space ceases to exist. This is something else. A dreaming palace of wonders. A hall of light and sound. Surprisingly, as it has so rightly been said, this is not just a palace at night, but rather a palace night and day, equally so by artificial light and by daylight. At the same time, it is not a light-box where the light obliterates space, or a hollow drum without objects. There are the group of figures by Miquel Blay (mentioned above) the busts of the great classical composers (Palestrina, Bach, Beethoven, Wagner) not to mention the marvellous group of mosaics, presided over by the one by Lluís Bru representing the Orfeó Català. And the effect overall here, as in other buildings by Domènech i Montaner, reminds one of the depths of the sea. A magic sea teeming with rocks, pebbles, starfish, flowers, colours, lights and reflectors. A magic fishbowl.

Miquel Blay's sculptural group
Old Barcelona seen from the Palau roof ➲

Allegoric mosaic of the Orfeó Català on the front of the building, by Lluís Bru, based on a drawing by Lluís Domènech i Montaner

The busts of Palestrina, Bach, Beethoven and Wagner grace the front of the building

ᴄ Central female figure of the mosaic on the main façade

Modernist façade

The old ticket office, decorated with Lluís Bru mosaics

THE VESTIBULE AND THE STAIRS

The interior of the building is even more extraordinary than the exterior. The portico with two arches, supported by a massive pillar was formerly used as the entrance and a covered area for those arriving by car, to protect them from the weather. Almost immediately next to this is the ticket office with its six concentric arches made of different materials, as well as a myriad combination of pastel colours and floral shapes. And below that the name of the mosaic artist, Lluís Bru. On the other side, the main entrance for the public.

The ceiling of the vestibule is decorated with geometrically arranged glazed ceramic mouldings, with lights, forming star-shaped patterns. Three steps are enough to separate the vestibule from a second area beginning on either side with lamps on a tall base and short column, which serve to highlight the transparent open space, bathing all in light. Before restoration was carried out, there was a stained glass window at the far end with the Orfeó Català crest, now the door to the foyer.

To the left and right, two marble staircases emerge, beginning with crowned lamps on columns. The banisters are also marble supported by transparent yellow glass balusters. The wide tread of each stair makes walking up to the first floor easy, while the underside of the stairs forms a canopy of gleaming tiles for the vestibule.

The vestibule in a 360-degree panoramic view

The vestibule and the stairs

Detail of main marble staircase, with transparent yellow glass balusters

44

Floral motifs are typical of the decor throughout the Palau

View of the staircase and the vestibule bathed in welcoming lamplight

THE LLUÍS MILLET LOUNGE

On the first floor there is the salon named in honour of Lluís Millet, an area where concert-goers can rest or arrange to meet. Here there are busts or statues of other personalities connected with the Palau. From floor to ceiling, the lounge is two floors high, with ornate floral stained glass windows that are of exceptional artistic quality. Even more extraordinary is the way the double colonnade on the front of the building is seen more clearly from this angle, looking through the windows, than from the street. Every column is coloured and decorated differently, contributing much to the originality and attraction of the feature. It is hardly surprising, therefore, that this lounge is considered one of the finest rooms in the Palau.

Lluís Millet Lounge

Looking down on the lounge is the *mestre* himself

Columns, main balcony

Columns decorated with floral motifs in varied shapes and colours

Details of column mosaics

THE CONCERT HALL

"The concert hall," wrote David Mackay, "is one of the most beautiful in the world (...) without exaggeration, it is one of its most important architectural treasures. Its space, simple, complex, mystical and paradoxical, defies accurate description."

The concert hall is rectangular as is the space cut out of the ceiling from which is suspended the great light in the shape of a giant drop. The drop-shaped light contrasts with the straight lines, all the straight lines in the ceiling; as if all the straight lines and rectangles wanted to stop the fantastic luminous drop, with its exuberant colour and light, from finally dropping. That the hanging light should suggest an inverted dome is a paradox. Here, the positive and negative exist side by side, they interplay, complement and contrast one another.

The wonderful skylight inevitably attracts one's gaze: A sun, a kindly sun in shades of gold, which sheds light but does not burn. It is made up of little suns of different sizes, like a galaxy. The background sky, on the

other hand, is dark, lighter where it expands. It is like a lake, reflecting the sun, moving in waves, waves that are girls, girls that are sprites, sprites singing in the water; those closest to the sun are fair, further out, some are fair and some are dark. A heavenly choir of ladies of the lake.

These water sprites, as we shall see in a moment when talking about the figures, find their echo in the damsels playing musical instruments ranged round the back of the stage: the latter are like sirens, with solid upper halves that stand out from the wall, and skirts drawn in stones in soft underwater hues.

This architectural art is brimming over with solutions, ideas, imagination. Everything has been carefully thought out, for its utility, for its originality, for its charm, for its rhythm, for its beauty. The concert hall artists make their entrance onto the stage through a high narrow pointed archway – or rather they used to: since the renovation, this entrance is not used. For that reason the artists have to (or rather had to) come onto the stage in sin-

gle file. As if to say, "we are entering as individuals, but when we sing we will be a choir – something more than, and different from, the sum of the parts."

This auditorium is unique. It is not a theatre: the sculptures make the use of scenery impractical. It is not a church despite the organ and despite the apse-end of the building with its figures; the religion here is pagan. It is a concert hall with the impertinent, not to say distracting, presence of the sculptures. It brings to mind the drawing rooms of wealthy nobles where music was played, and the listeners sat around in armchairs surrounded by paintings, statues, vases, lights, glass cases full of jewels and trinkets. They listened to music because they wanted to. Because it brought it all together. This, then, is a concert hall which resembles a theatre, a chapel, a drawing room. But in reality it is something else – a modernist concert hall. Modernism, after all, excels in transcending conventional spaces. And this is the culminating masterpiece of its author.

Entrance to second floor ➲

Winged horse: sculpture in white stone

The fabulous auditorium ➲

The concert hall organ

The apse-ended stage, framed by large sculptures ➲

Stained-glass windows of the side façade adorned with garlands of flowers

The skylight in the shape of an enormous drop of light

Skylight: Detail showing colours

With the skylight overhead, the drop becomes a fiery sun ➲

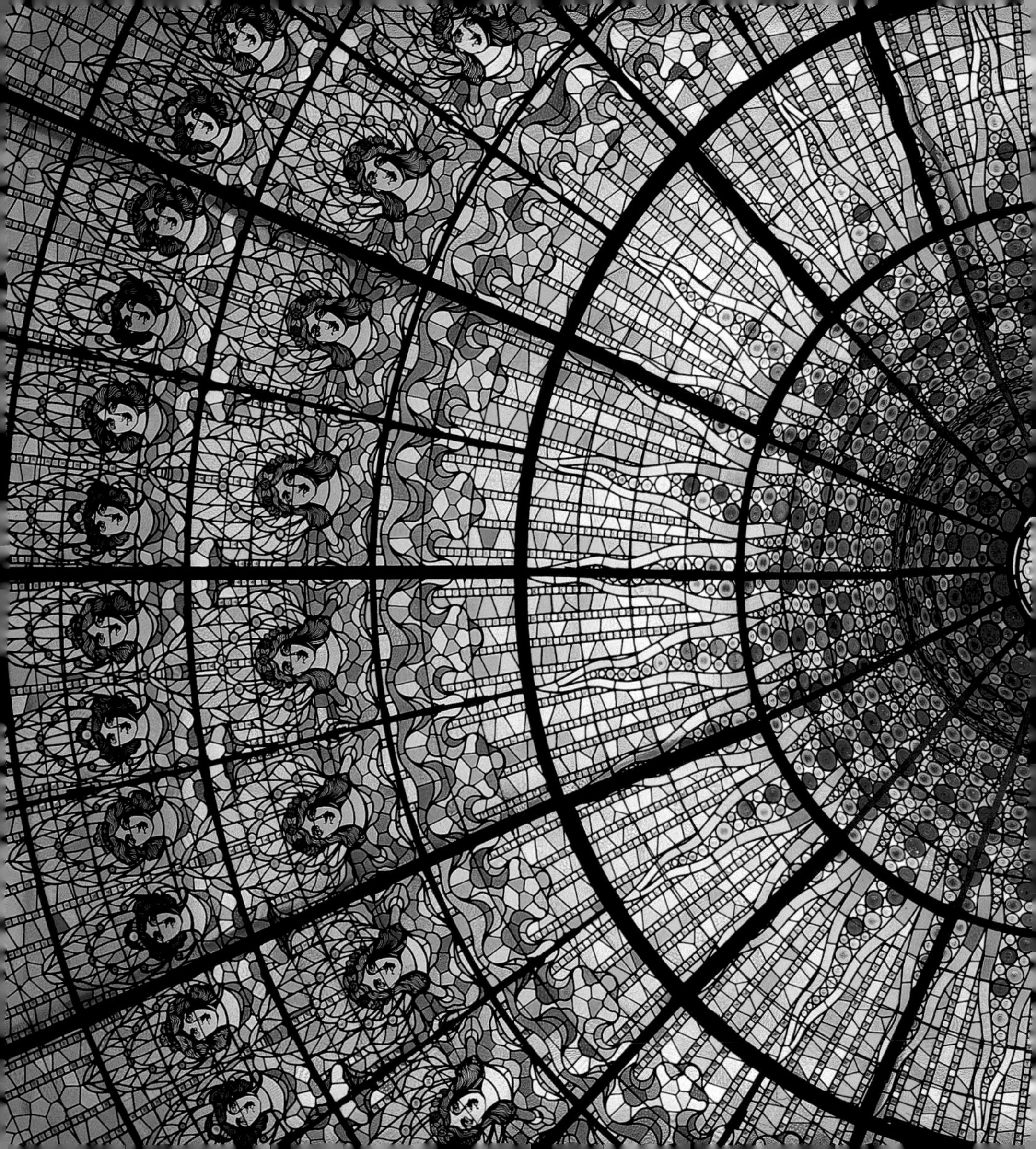

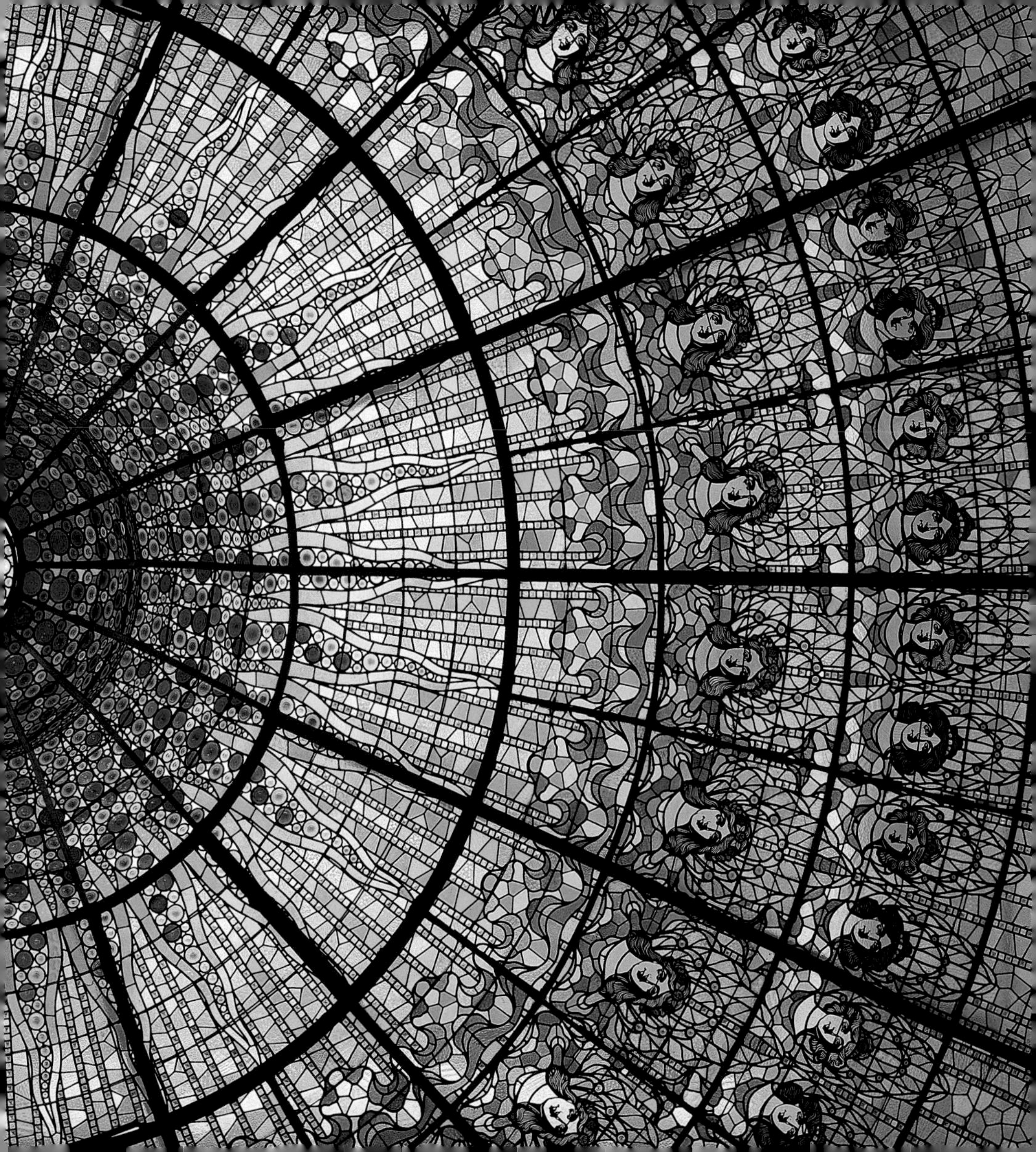

Eccentrically hung crowns, second floor balcony of the concert hall

THE SCULPTURES

he Palau's main raison d'être is music of all types, and the programmes have reflected this variety since the outset. Yet Lluís Domènech i Montaner gave primacy to choral singing in the decor, probably with Lluís Millet's tacit agreement. The celestial choir of young women encircling the hanging light above the concert hall make this clear. And so does the figure of Josep Anselm Clavé on the left of the stage. Clavé, with his famous choirs, epitomises the popular choral style, a style that was promoted better than anyone by the Orpheon societies. It is probably true to say that, artistically speaking, the Orfeó Català was the most ambitious of all the Orpheons in Catalonia. The idea is seen again in the girls seated beneath Clavé's pedestal, singing "Les Flors de Maig" and united in a choir of glorious voices. Yet another instance is the great arch over the front of the stage, with the figures by sculptors Dídac Masana and Pablo Gargallo. The latter represent the ride of the Valkyries, act three, scene one of The Valkyrie by Wagner, where the female voice choir takes on extraordinary musical power. Beethoven's bust, on the right side of the stage, can be seen in this light as a tribute to classical music and its culmination in the human voice: the music and words of the "Ode to Joy" by Schiller, in the Ninth Symphony.

Winged horse
"The flowers of May" ➲

Notwithstanding, the figures generally seen as the peak of the Palau's achievements and its most attractive artistic feature are not a choir of human voices, but rather a strictly musical group. These are the damsels who appear against the background to the stage. Eighteen in all, nine on each side, they were sculpted by Eusebi Arnau where they project from the wall. Mario Maragliano (according to some) or Lluís Bru (according to others) made their lower halves formed by mosaic work. Apparently they were given a hostile reception by the critics during the early days, while now they are admired by everyone. There is no doubt that the sculptures, with their variety of different blouses and headdresses have vivacious charm. The mosaics depicting their waists, skirts, feet and shoes in different styles from different places, are delicate and incredibly heraldic in their simplicity. They represent an accomplished group of musicians playing popular and orchestral instruments.

The horses that dominate the upper balcony represent Pegasus, the winged horse that sprang, according to Greek myth, from the union of Poseidon and Medusa. Pegasus was ridden by the Muses when the gods – especially Zeus – called them. Zeus wanted them by his side on Olympus, where they could sing the wonders of the world to the satisfaction of the celestial court.

The Valkiries ➲

Bust of Josep Anselm Clavé

Bust of Beethoven

The Palau emblem at the top of Procenium arch

C The figures by the sculptor Eusebi Arnau emerge from the wall of the semicircular theatre

Tenth of April, 1905: beginning of the works

C Although they do not correspond to the nine daughters of Zeus, goddesses of song and dance, the eighteen figures of the semicircular theatre are popularly known as The Muses

Details of the figures and mosaics

"Medieval" fabulous beast, at entrance to the second floor

◉ The mosaics forming part of the figures

THE DECORATIVE ARTS

T he Palau de la Música is in itself an ode to joy. There must be few buildings in the world where joy is more resplendent. To forget or ignore this is to miss half the Palau's significance. One only has to see the ceramic-clad columns of the first floor of the façade, with their startling range of colours, plant forms, arabesques, and their combination of materials, to realise that no other style ever succeeded on this level as the Palau de la Música has so consummately succeeded in doing.

The Palau, then, is an exceptional piece of work in terms of the originality of the structure and new ways of handling space. In addition to that, however, the Palau is outstanding in its utilisation of industrial techniques. As was mentioned earlier, Domènech i Montaner had already opened a workshop in one of his own buildings, the Castell dels tres Dragons. The role of this workshop was to teach the application of arts to architecture, with the assistance of the architect Gallissà. This interest is very evident when one looks at the Palau, in the different ways of working ceramics, glass, iron and other metals, and wood.

Ceramics are found throughout the building: floors, banisters, ceilings, decorating the walls, the columns, the ticket office, the auditorium. It appears in almost all colours, tones, now painted, now glazed.

The mosaic artists were Lluís Bru, a ceramics artist and scenographer from Alicante in south-east Spain, and Mario Maragliano, a Genovese who gave up music for ceramics and worked in Barcelona until his death. Also involved were certain specialist firms, for example Pujol & Baucis, and Escofet & Cia.

The stained glass are by specialist firms, the most famous being Rigalt Granell. The architect who was in overall charge was Fransesc Guàrdia i Vidal, Domènech i Montaner's son-in-law.

Capital with wreath of pine cones and leaves in the concert hall
Pegasus, winged horse of classical mythology ➲

Details of the ceramics

Mosaics in varied colours and shapes ➲

106

Colourful stained glass with floral and musical motifs

The texture of the glass filters the light into many colours

THE FOYER

At the far end of the vestibule are the doors that open onto what were formerly the Society's headquarters. This area has been renovated and is now the bar and foyer (concert hall lounge and other uses). A large number of people can be accommodated around the tables both during concerts and when the area is used as an independent restaurant.

Here, the wide brick arches are more sober, less exuberant, but they are attractively decorated with lines of glazed green ceramics and flowers – also ceramic – in pinks and light yellows. The ceiling broadly speaking repeats the ornamentation used with the other ceilings in the Palau. As a result of the Tusquets renovation, it is the floor that most clearly departs from the materials, shapes and colours used originally by Domènech i Montaner and by modernist architects in general. What Tusquets was looking for in the carpets and new objects, however, were contrasts that were equivalent, albeit at a different level, to those found in the variety of colours used by Domènech i Montaner.

This large space features a remodelling of the bar counter, fitted between four columns, and reminiscent of modernist offices in Barcelona's Eixample district. The coloured glass seems to wink back at the panes that form the great light hanging over the auditorium.

Because of the importance of the massive pillars, we see the combination of exposed brick and ceramic decoration here, in the foyer, better than in any other part of the Palau. The ceramic ornaments are sometimes glazed tiles and sometimes ceramic flowers clinging to the capitals and indeed almost replacing them.

On display in a glass case there is the Society's banner designed by Antoni Maria Gallisà, with the crest of the Society embroidered on the back on modernist fabric. The year the Society was founded is also shown: 1891. And in another case are the names of the patrons and the members of the Foundation (Fundació Orfeó Català-Palau de la Música Catalana).

The foyer in a 360-degree panoramic view

Standard of the Orfeó Català designed by Antoni M. Gallissà and table designed by Domènech i Montaner

Detail of a bench

The foyer, on the ground floor, is a renovated area ➲

The Foyer bar

Flowers in impressionist style decorate these capitals

Foyer ceiling, with green ceramic ribbing

Gothic-inspired star vaulting

Exposed brickwork combined with ceramic decoration on pillars

Stained glass partition between foyer and vestibule ➲

View of the Foyer from the vestibule

The Modernist western façade had remained hidden for nearly half a century

Lounge and bar, on the second floor; columns and ceiling utilising subtle forms

The old door to the chamber music hall

The renovated chamber music room

The first stone, placed on the 23rd of April 1905

Ceramic support ➲

REMODELLING AND EXTENSION WORKS. 1982–1989

The remodelling and extension works on the Palau, entrusted to the architects Oscar Tusquets and Carles Díaz, began in 1982 and were completed with the official opening in 1989. They have been described as exemplary and as a result the Palau de la Música has recovered its original state and at the same time expanded its space, thus increasing its possibilities.

Additionally, the successful remodelling work is based on the fact that they have used the brick, stone, stained glass mosaic, glass and iron in a similar way to how Domènech i Montaner himself used the materials, although with the essential adaptations to the building's new uses. Furthermore, if before the Palau was boxed between dividing walls, the remodelling and extension has provided it with vital space, above all due to the reduction of the neighbouring church and to the creation of a small square in the rear part, enabling comfortable access to the new building and the entry of both air and light.

Besides the technical improvements, which were perhaps the most essential, those that genuinely attract one's attention are the ones that have affected the building's appearance. The creation of an outer stairway, between the church and the Palau, has meant that it can now be seen almost as a box surrounded on all sides by light, like a "music box", unrestricted and in free movement. The semicircular theatre where the choir and musicians are placed has been similarly expanded, enriched with the improvement in acoustics, a fundamental element in halls devoted to music and the spoken word.

Finally, the construction of an adjoining building of six floors for dressing rooms, library and archive, represents the appropriate expansion that the Palau de la Música needed so much.

Office vestibule in a 360-degree panoramic view

Tower, new building, with unusual glass crown

"Orfeó Català" legend over new building entrance

Foot of tower, adorned with palm fronds

The Orfeó Català library

Skylight illuminating the stage

Offices occupy the upper storeys of the Palau, above the concert hall. Originally, this area was Lluís Millet's apartment ➲

THE PALAU IN THE 21ST CENTURY

After the works of the first enlargement and reform of the Palau (1983-1989), Oscar Tusquets began a new enlargement stage (1999-2004) that once again took into account both the respect for the work by Domènech i Montaner and the contribution of innovative solutions.

This new stage consisted of the construction of an underground auditorium, a building adjoining the main façade and a public square; new spaces that were made possible by the transfer of the parish church of Sant Francesc.

This enlargement represents the completion of the Palau, because it enables the toothing that broke the rectangular regularity of the building to be eliminated and also allows the beauty of the western glass façade to be fully appreciated, hidden from view since the Palau was opened in 1908, and only open in part after the remodelling works that were completed in 1989.

The architectural category of the project, the total harmony with the Modernist Palau and the creative power of the façade of the new building –based on the technique of sculpted brick, according to the design by Oscar Tusquets– gives the entire building an image of dignity and importance.

The old dream of Domènech i Montaner has come true and the Palau de la Música Catalana can finally be seen and admired in all its splendour.

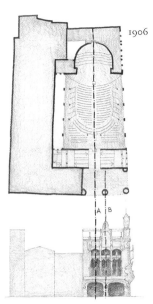
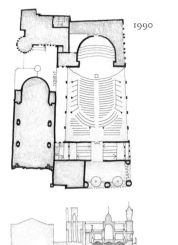
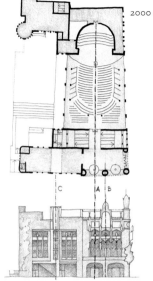

1906   1990   2000

Urban development of the Palau block and model showing the square and the façades with the underground Petit Palau

SQUARE AND FAÇADES

With the creation of a public square, on occasions the setting for open-air concerts, the urban facilities of this district in Barcelona, so devoid of open spaces, have been considerably improved, while also providing the perspective required to be able to take in the side façade designed by Domènech i Montaner.

The square has been closed off on its south side by a new building that extends the main façade while also giving it continuity in its linking with the western side façade.

This new building, through which the Petit Palau, the new underground auditorium, is reached, is for public use and has a rooftop restaurant and different multifunctional spaces in line with the current demands for this kind of cultural and leisure facility.

On the new façade by Oscar Tusquets, as well as the use of brick and glass, we come across other echoes, or homages, to the building by Domènech i Montaner, whether because of its rounded form, which sends us messages of a Modernist corner, or for the twenty-two metre high engraving of the tree that recalls the willow of the proscenium arch of the stage.

View of the Palau square

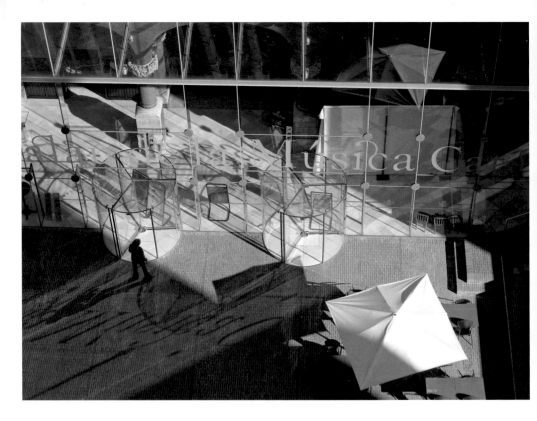

The square framed by the recovered western façade

The sculpture of Lluís Millet overlooks the square

Restaurant Mirador

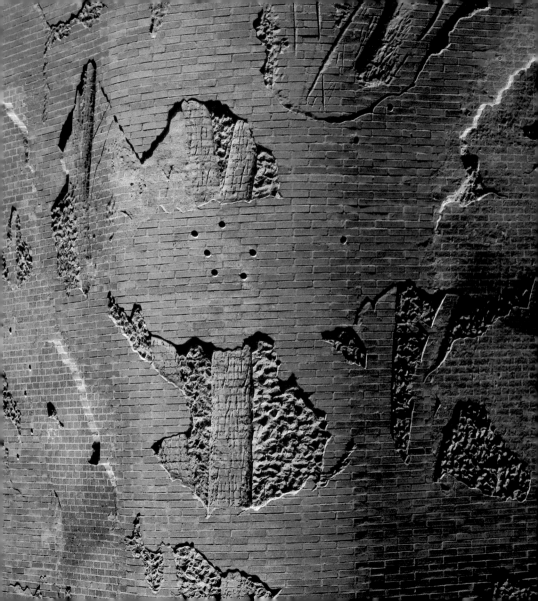

The façade with the twenty-two metre high tree engraved in the façade

THE PETIT PALAU

Beneath the square, 11 metres deep, the Petit Palau was opened in 2004. The new auditorium has a capacity for 538 people with a variable acoustic for all kinds of concerts and with the latest technology in audiovisual facilities.

Its optimum acoustic conditions make it the ideal space for lied concerts, concerts for chamber music and choirs, jazz, etc. Moreover, the stalls have retractable seats that can be stored beneath the stage, giving it a great deal of flexibility in terms of cultural or social uses, such as conferences, symposiums, conventions...

On the other hand, although the Petit Palau is a 21st century hall in terms of concept and technology, the spirit of Domènech i Montaner remains in the treatment of light and transparencies, enabling the auditorium to be both a warm and modern space at the same time.

The entrance stairway of the Petit Palau

Concert hall of the Petit Palau ➲

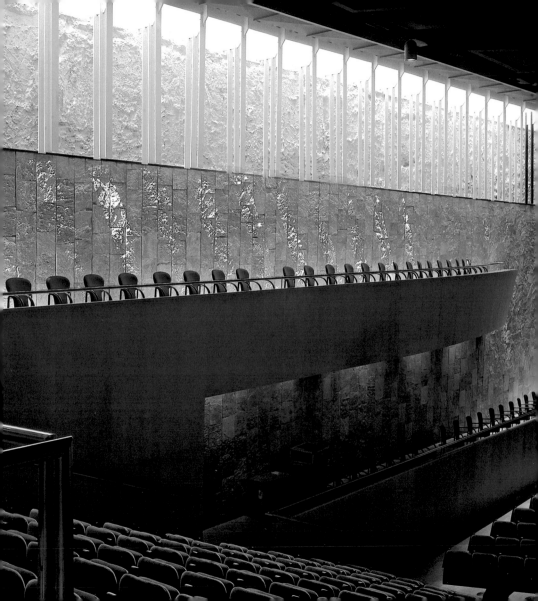